Artlist Collection

THE PIG™

Pigalicious

■SCHOLASTIC

www.thepig-club.com

THIS IS A CARLTON BOOK

Published in 2011 by Carlton Books Limited
20 Mortimer Street
London W1T 3JW

The Pig Logo and Photographs © artlist 2011
Design © Carlton Books Limited 2011
Text © Scholastic Inc. 2011
Text by Tori Kosara

10 9 8 7 6 5 4 3 2 1   11 12 13 14 15

ISBN 978-0-545-32719-0

JFMAMJJASO D/2010/6668
Printed in Dongguan, China
First printing, January 2011

 # Oink-troduction

We pigs are lovable, playful, and very cute (you could say we're PIGALICIOUS)! Even though we enjoy cooling off in the mud, pigs are some of the cleanest animals around, and we make great pets. Playful pigs have lived with happy humans for thousands of years, and even some of today's top celebrities love having piggy pets. But we are more than supercute, we are also supersmart. Scientists have proven that pigs are more intelligent than dogs (did you know we can play computer games with our sensational snouts?).

Even if you don't have a pig of your own, these pretty piggy pictures are sure to put a smile on your face. From snout to curly tail, pigs are totally worth squealing about.

A baby pig is called a piglet.
Piglets drink milk until they are old
enough to eat with grown-up pigs.

 More milk, please!

Pretty in pink.

Female pigs are called sows,
and male pigs are boars.

He's boring.

 "Sow" what?

Pigs have stout bodies and are
covered with coarse hair.

 Does this look like
my natural color?

 Lookin' good!

Pigs come in many different colors. Small Yorkshire pigs are snowy white, while Poland China pigs are black and white, and Duroc pigs are red.

This looks good in any color.

I'm shopping for something that goes with my hair.

Pigs love to be clean! Because we can't sweat, we roll in the mud to cool off. But we aren't really dirty!

 Ah, bathtime is the best.

Clean and ready for a nap.

Did you know that pigs can suffer from sunburn? That's another reason we like to roll in the mud and hang out in the shade.

I should be safe from the sun in here!

 Ah! The sun sure feels good, but I don't want to get burned.

Pigs have four toes on each foot, but they only walk on the larger, middle two toes.

Do you want to see my dance moves?

 I've been on my feet all day!

Our supersensitive snouts help us find yummy food, such as fruit, worms, and grass!

 I don't smell anything to eat here!

 Do you like my new hairstyle?

Sometimes people use us
to help them sniff out things
that they can't find.

Mmm ... these
flowers smell sweet!

 Does my snout
look big to you?

We can make lots of different sounds ("oink oink"). Pigs can squeal, roar, and snort – very loudly!

Are you sure you can hear me?

I LOVE to sing!

Pigs have really good eyesight and a great sense of hearing.

 Look into my eye.

No need to shout.
I hear you!

Did someone say *party*? Pigs
are very social and like to be
around lots of other pigs.

 I'm ready to party!

 Does this outfit look okay?

Pigs make good friends.
We love to play with
other piggies.

🐷 Let's play hide-and-seek.

Can we play, too?

We pigs often greet our
friends by touching snouts.

 M-wah!

Have you met my
snuggly duck friend?

31

Pigs also love to snuggle with
their friends at bedtime.

 You're hogging the
whole basket!

Nighty-night.

Pigs are curious animals. We like to listen to music, play with balls, and keep busy.

 What? I'm not supposed to be in here?

34

Play ball?

Pigs can also be brave. Once a pig even saved a boy from drowning!

It's safe to swim while I'm here.

Does this scarf look like a superhero cape?

Wild pigs are strong and fierce, and like to live in forests.

Argh! Watch out, matey, I'm a wild pirate pig.

Aloha! What do you mean I don't look tough?

The smallest kind of pig is called the Mini Maialino, and grows to be only about 20 pounds (9 kg). So far, the biggest pig in history weighed over 2,000 pounds (907 kg)!

 This basket is just my size.

I'm taller than
you are!

One of the priciest pigs
was sold for $56,000
in March 1985.

It's a tough life, but
someone has to do it.

I need more diamonds for my cell phone.

Did you know that pigs
can run a mile in just
seven minutes?

🐷 Whew! I'm
exhausted.

I'm running …
… for Queen!

We pigs have the highest IQ of any common house pet. It's even easier to train us than to try to teach dogs or cats new tricks.

Only the best and the brightest piggy princesses rule this kingdom.

Quite right,
Princess Piggy!

Now that you know how cute, playful,
clean, smart, and lovable we pigs
are, we hope you agree that
we're totally PIGALICIOUS
from snout to tail!

Excuse me.
I said no
photos, please.